THE CHILULAS

ELAINE LANDAU

THE CHILULAS

Franklin Watts   New York   Chicago   London   Toronto   Sydney   A First Book

Map by Joe LeMonnier
Cover photograph copyright©: Ben Klaffke

Photographs copyright ©: Ben Klaffke: pp. 3, 12, 19, 22, 23, 26, 28, 29, 32, 34, 38, 41, 44, 54; National Museum of the American Indian, Smithsonian Institution: pp. 16, 21, 36, 46; California State University, Chico, Meriam Library, Special Collections: pp. 17, 47; North Wind Picture Archives, Alfred, Me.: pp. 50, 53.

Library of Congress Cataloging-in-Publication Data

Landau, Elaine.
The Chilulas / by Elaine Landau.
p. cm. — (A First book)
Includes bibliographical references and index.
ISBN 0-531-20132-5 (lib. bdg.) — ISBN 0-531-15685-0 (pbk.)
1. Chilula Indians—History—Juvenile literature. 2. Chilula Indians—Social life and customs—Juvenile literature. [1. Chilula Indians. 2. Indians of North America.] I. Title. II. Series.
E99.C553L35 1994
979.4'004972—dc20   93-31423 CIP AC

CONTENTS

OTHER BOOKS BY ELAINE LANDAU

BILL CLINTON

THE CHEROKEES

COLIN POWELL: FOUR STAR GENERAL

COWBOYS

DYSLEXIA

ENDANGERED PLANTS

THE HOPI

INTERESTING INVERTEBRATES:
A LOOK AT SOME ANIMALS WITHOUT BACKBONES

JUPITER

LYME DISEASE

MARS

NAZI WAR CRIMINALS

NEPTUNE

THE POMO

THE RIGHT TO DIE

SATURN

STATE BIRDS:
INCLUDING THE COMMONWEALTH OF PUERTO RICO

STATE FLOWERS:
INCLUDING THE COMMONWEALTH OF PUERTO RICO

THE SIOUX

SURROGATE MOTHERS

TROPICAL RAIN FORESTS AROUND THE WORLD

WE HAVE AIDS

WE SURVIVED THE HOLOCAUST

A Note about the Photographs

By the mid-1800s the Chilulas no longer existed as a distinct people but had merged with their neighbors the Hupa Indians. It was a likely blend because in numerous ways the groups were the same. As photographs of the Chilulas are unavailable, this book has been largely illustrated with pictures of the Hupas.

THE CHILULAS

A PATH THROUGH WHAT WAS ONCE CHILULA INDIAN TERRITORY.
THE CHILULAS FELT A SPECIAL BOND TO THE TALL REDWOODS.

THE CHILULA INDIANS

Centuries before Europeans came to America, a group of between five and six hundred American Indians lived in a small part of what is now northwest California. They occupied the lower portion of the Redwood Creek basin. To their west was a thick blanket of tall magnificent redwood trees. To the east were the Bald Hills — a series of ridges with nearly treeless tops. Summers there were cool, while winters tended to be rainy but mild.

These people lived in close harmony with nature. They viewed the land and its bounty as special gifts that were not to be abused. They were the Chilula Indians, people who believed that everything on Earth had its purpose.

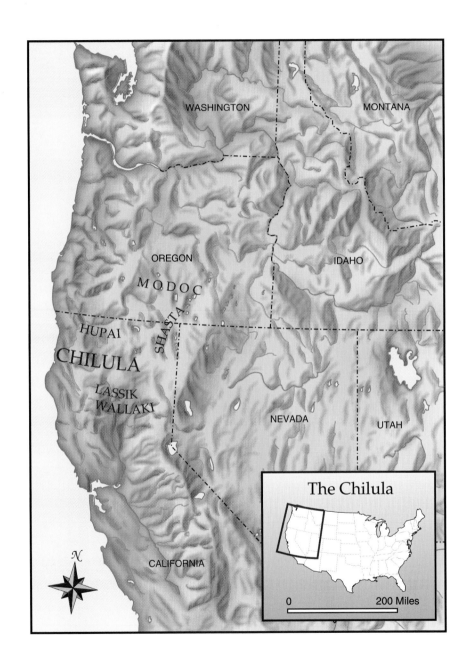

WASHINGTON

MONTANA

OREGON

IDAHO

MODOC

SHASTA

HUPAI

CHILULA

LASSIK
WALLAKI

NEVADA

UTAH

CALIFORNIA

N

The Chilula

0   200 Miles

CHILULA VILLAGES AND FAMILIES

Groups of Chilula Indians lived in small villages scattered throughout the area. Each contained about thirty people. Most of these settlements were on the east side of Redwood Creek. It was sunnier there and the trees were less dense. The Chilulas also had temporary camps in the Bald Hills, where they stayed during the summer and fall. They usually chose sites high on a ridge near a cool brook or stream.

The Chilulas' permanent homes in Redwood Creek basin were square structures made of redwood slabs. The houses were built over dug-out pits. A notched plank served as a stairway leading down to them. Near the pit's center, a scooped-out area bordered by stones was used for a fire. A family's food

THE CHILULAS BUILT THEIR HOMES OUT OF REDWOOD SLABS.
SMALL PIECES OF LEFTOVER WOOD WERE USED TO MAKE DRUM
FRAMES, MEDICINE BOXES, AND OTHER ITEMS.

CHILULA MEN USED THE SWEATHOUSE (SHOWN ABOVE) BEFORE GOING
ON A HUNT. INSIDE, OLDER MEN TOLD YOUNG BOYS ANCIENT HUNTING
STORIES AND EXPLAINED THE RELIGIOUS LAWS GOVERNING THE HUNT.

supplies, personal articles, and kindling for fires were stored in their home.

Besides these dwellings, a Chilula community also contained *sweathouses*. These rectangular redwood buildings were constructed over dug-out pits as well. Steam in the sweathouses was provided by pouring hot water over stones. Sweating was considered an important purification rite. It was done by Chilula men before special rituals and ceremonies as well as at other times. Many Chilula villages also had a round ceremonial redwood dance house.

Chilula society revolved around the family. The average family consisted of a husband and wife, their children, and perhaps a grandparent or other relative. Usually related families lived near one another in separate households. These groups often worked together and acted as a unit even though there was no official village chief or ruling council. Some Chilula villages were made up of several extended families. In the smaller villages, however, just about everybody was related to everybody else.

Children were an important part of Chilula life. Pregnant women carefully watched their diets so that their infants would be healthy. At first a newborn remained with its mother. When the baby was ten days old it was wrapped in deerskin cloth and placed in a basket cradle. The child wasn't named until he or

BABY BASKETS LIKE THIS ONE WERE WOVEN BY CHILULA
WOMEN. THE BASKETS MADE COMFORTABLE CRADLES
AND CARRIERS FOR THEIR YOUNG.

she was five years old. Until that time the youngster was referred to by an affectionate term such as "small one" or "little boy."

Young people spent much of their time playing although all were schooled in their people's customs and ways. Girls learned to weave baskets and gather berries and herbs by watching their mothers. Boys were taught to hunt and fish by their fathers and uncles.

When a Chilula girl turned fifteen or sixteen she might marry a boy who was seventeen or eighteen. Although these native people lived in villages of extended families, a young person was not permitted to marry a close relative. There was no formal Chilula wedding ceremony. A feast was simply held and the bride's and groom's families exchanged gifts. From then on the couple were considered husband and wife. They usually made their home in the groom's village.

The Chilulas were extremely aware of wealth and status. Among them wealth might take the form of shell currency (money), desirable housing sites or hunting and gathering areas, white or other unusually colored animal skins, and various other special items.

Wealth was a sign of rank and influence in the village. Rich men were respected and looked up to.

CHILDREN AND FAMILY LIFE WERE IMPORTANT TO THE
CHILULAS. BOYS AND GIRLS WERE TAUGHT THEIR PEOPLE'S
CUSTOMS AT AN EARLY AGE.

UNLIKE THE COIN AND PAPER MONEY WE USE, THE
CHILULAS FASHIONED THEIR CURRENCY OUT OF
SHELLS SUCH AS THESE.

While it was supposedly possible to acquire riches
through hard work, wealth was usually passed on
through families.

Wealth was also a factor when marriage partners
for young people were selected. Well-off families
wanted the bride's or groom's family to be similar in

CHILULA WOMEN WOVE A VARIETY OF BASKETS. AT TIMES THEY MADE
A RED DYE FROM THE BARK OF THE ALDER TREE TO COLOR THEM.

status. When a young man married, he had to come up with an agreed-upon bridal price. This might be paid in either shell money or with other desirable gifts. In turn, young Chilula brides came to the marriage with a *dowry* consisting of necessary household articles.

FOOD

The Chilulas lived off the land. Men hunted the abundant elk and deer that roamed the redwood forest bordering the west side of the basin. Often the Chilulas hunted in groups. Although the older, more experienced men led the way, young boys frequently came along to learn to track and kill these animals.

Before going off on a hunt the men entered the sweathouse to spiritually cleanse or purify themselves. The bows, arrows, knives, and scrapers to be used on the animal were cleansed as well. The hunters prayed for success and burned special roots as an offering. Such offerings were made to the hunted animal's spirit in return for its life and flesh.

HERE, FISH CAUGHT BY PRESENT-DAY AMERICAN
INDIANS ARE CURED IN A SMOKEHOUSE. IN EARLY
TIMES, CHILULAS ALSO SMOKED SOME OF THEIR FISH
AND MEAT FOR LATER USE.

The freshly killed elk or deer was brought back to the village. After it was roasted over an open fire, the Indians ate their fill. The remaining meat was cut into strips and dried. It was stored and eaten at a later time.

Like many California Indians, the Chilulas believed in land ownership and private property. Numerous hunting sites were owned by individuals or families. Only the property owners could use the land belonging to them.

Although hunting was more important to the Chilulas than fishing, the Indians also fished in Redwood Creek. They caught salmon, trout, candle-fish, and others. Sometimes they threw brush fences across the creek to trap fish swimming downstream. On other occasions, they used a hook and line, scooped the fish into baskets, or even caught them with their hands. When the water level was low they drugged the fish with the soaproot plant to slow them down, making them easier to catch.

In addition, the Chilulas caught and ate eels from the creek. Sometimes they speared them in the water with *harpoons* made from elk and deer *antlers*. Eels were also trapped in eel pots — basketlike traps the Indians wove from hazel and willow tree sticks. The fish and eels they caught might be eaten right away or dried and stored for later.

THE CHILULAS SOMETIMES DRUGGED FISH WITH THE
SOAPROOT PLANT. THIS SLOWED THE FISH DOWN,
MAKING THEM EASIER TO CATCH. THE INDIANS USED
SOAPROOT FOR OTHER PURPOSES AS WELL.

THE CHILULAS OFTEN WOVE BASKETLIKE TRAPS
SUCH AS THIS ONE TO CATCH FISH.

Foods gathered in the wild were also extremely important to these native people's survival. Before having contact with whites, the Chilulas did not grow or cultivate gardens or crops. Instead they learned to make use of a wide assortment of plant foods that the girls and women picked by hand in the wild.

In the late summer and early fall, while at their temporary camps, they found many different types of berries. Among these were huckleberries, strawberries, salmonberries, and others. After collecting them, the berries were sorted, cleaned, cooked, and preserved. Males used huckleberry shoots to make their arrows and often gathered this arrowwood just before the winter set in.

The large number of wild ferns growing in northern California also served the Indians well. While some ferns were boiled and made into soups and teas by the Chilulas, others were used in basketmaking or to preserve foods. Chilula men wrapped meat and fish in certain types of ferns before going on a journey. This helped keep the food fresh until they reached their destination.

Every fall the Chilulas dug for wild potatoes. Although these were usually cooked over a hot fire, they were also eaten raw. Indian lettuce, sometimes called miner's lettuce, was gathered from the same area and eaten raw as well. Clover was also picked and used both in tea or as a salad. Chilula women were experts at identifying numerous seeds, wild oats, and grasses that were healthful and abundant.

Acorns were considered essential to the Chilulas' food supply. The Indians gathered them near the end of autumn. After being collected, dried, and shelled, the women ground these nuts in baskets. Later on they would pour cold water over the acorn flour to remove its bitter flavor. When acorn mush or soup was needed, they cooked the flour in special water-tight baskets.

The Chilulas also collected various wild plants and herbs to use as medicines. They brewed plants such as the princess pine and the Oregon grape to make healing teas. These liquids were believed to help those suffering from kidney, gallbladder, and liver problems as well as other ailments.

Wild onions were sometimes eaten, but were also used to make soothing *poultices*. They were applied to relieve insect stings and bites. Yarrow, still another plant, was also made into poultices and applied to cuts, sores, and certain types of rashes. At times yarrow was boiled and used to make a healing drink as well. Like Chilula hunting grounds, various gathering areas were considered the private property of

NUTS WERE AN IMPORTANT FOOD SOURCE FOR THE
CHILULAS. NATIVE WOMEN WERE KNOWLEDGEABLE
ABOUT GROWING SEASONS AND GATHERING AREAS.

individuals or families. These owners usually set up
their temporary summer and fall camps near their
property.

DRESS

Northern California's somewhat mild climate influenced how the Chilulas dressed. Most of the time they didn't need heavy clothing. Instead the men usually wore only a *breechclout* made of deerskin or other available animal skins.

The women wore two-piece buckskin skirts that extended below the knees. At times Chilula women also wore dresses made of maplewood bark. The bark was pulled from maple trees in the early spring and pressed into a clothlike mass. Then it was cut and styled into a woman's dress.

On cooler days both Chilula men and women wrapped animal-skin robes around themselves. Most of the time the Chilulas went barefoot. Buckskin

ELABORATELY DECORATED DEERSKIN GARMENTS, SUCH AS
THIS ONE, WERE WORN DURING SPECIAL CEREMONIES.

moccasins, however, might be worn for protection on long trips. Hunters in areas where the brush was particularly thick also wore buckskin leggings. Males as well as females had their ears pierced and wore shell ornaments in them.

THE CHILULAS RESPECTED THE EARTH'S RESOURCES AND DID
NOT WASTE ANY PART OF THE ANIMALS THEY HUNTED. THEY
CARVED THESE SPOONS OUT OF ELK ANTLERS.

HANDIWORK

Although they had only a few crude tools to work with, Chilula men were excellent at woodworking. From the dense redwood forests they fashioned boards with which to build their homes and various chests to store personal, household, and ceremonial articles in. They also made hunting bows, bowls, small stools, pipes, and cedar headrests for the sweathouses.

In addition, the men made square drums by tightly stretching elk and deer hides over drum frames made of redwood. They carved various useful articles out of elk and deer horns as well. These included money boxes, wedges, simple tools, and spoons.

Women did the basket weaving. Their twine baskets and other woven items were usually made from

YOUNG CHILULA GIRLS LEARNED WEAVING FROM THEIR MOTHERS.
BESIDES MAKING VARIOUS TYPES OF BASKETS AND CONTAINERS,
THEY ALSO WOVE CAPS LIKE THE ONES SHOWN ABOVE.

hazel tree shoots. Besides baskets used to store items, these American Indian women also wove basket cradles, household articles, and caps, which they wore on their heads when carrying either heavy containers or a child in a cradle.

To add color to their baskets, the women sometimes used a red dye taken from the bark of the alder tree. They also relied on black maidenhair ferns and white bear grass to decorate their basket work.

ILLNESS AND HEALING

The Chilulas thought that serious illnesses were a result of supernatural causes. The stricken individual was generally not expected to recover on his own. In these instances, the services of a *shaman,* or healer, were required.

Most Chilula shamans were women believed to have extraordinary powers. Before treating a seriously ill patient, the shaman smoked a special pipe. Then she put her lips to the patient's skin and sucked until the harmful element was thought to have been drawn out of the ill person's body. A shaman was well paid for her work. These fees, however, were refunded if either the patient didn't improve soon or died within a short period of time.

YARROW WAS KNOWN AS A COMMON HEALING PLANT AMONG THE CHILULAS. THEY USED THE PLANT AS A POULTICE FOR WOUNDS, CUTS, AND SORES.

Even individuals with minor ailments sometimes called upon a shaman. In these cases, the shaman usually treated the person by giving him healing herbs and reciting a medicine formula. Some highly valued medicine formulas had been handed down through families in which there were a number of shamans.

A Chilula shaman was usually well off and looked up to within the community. Some shamans believed to be especially skilled and powerful became quite well known.

RELIGION

The Chilulas were very spiritual people. Their religious beliefs and practices were part of their daily life. They always tried to maintain a pure frame of mind, but this was especially crucial before such important undertakings as a hunt.

The Chilulas believed that god, or the Great Creator, was present in the earth, sky, and all of their physical surroundings. The redwood trees bordering their villages were sacred to them and seen as essential to their survival. The trees provided wood for their homes, medications, and even clothing fibers.

Feeling connected to the earth, the Chilulas lived in accord with nature. Their religious beliefs prohibited waste or misuse of the resources available to them. Following a deer or elk hunt, every part of the animal

THE REDWOODS, WHICH PROVIDED WOOD FOR CHILULA
SHELTERS, WERE SACRED TO THE INDIANS.

was used. The hides were scraped clean and made into cloaks, moccasins, blankets, knife covers, women's skirts, and other items. The deer's *sinews* were saved and later used as thread with which to sew garments. The sinews also served as cord. The elk's horns as well as its lower leg and ankle bones were fashioned into tools and other needed items.

At times special religious ceremonies were held to bring renewed life to the earth. These rituals were also performed to ward off hunger, illness, and other misfortunes. One such sacred ceremony was the White Deerskin Dance. It was held every summer or fall and lasted ten days. During this period the tale behind this ancient ritual was told. The males participating in the ceremony also danced while carrying either white or other unusually colored deerskins on top of long poles. Some dancers held sharpened blades covered with buckskin cloths as well.

When a Chilula Indian died special religious rituals were performed. The deceased's body was covered with a deerskin blanket and attached to a flat wooden plank. After being removed from the home through an opening in the wall, the words "You are going away from me. You must not think of me," were spoken. This was done to ensure that the dead person's spirit swiftly left the village and did not return from the dead. Then the corpse was placed in a shallow

THE WHITE DEERSKIN DANCE WAS ONE OF THE
CHILULA'S SACRED DANCES.

HERE A GROUP OF NATIVE PEOPLE ARE DRESSED TO PERFORM THE
WHITE DEERSKIN DANCE. NOTICE THE DEERSKINS ON THEIR POLES.

grave lined with wooden boards. A wide board put over the body completed the coffin.

The burial site was covered with earth and a few of the deceased's personal belongings were left on top. Relatives at a Chilula funeral often cried loudly, expressing their grief over their loved one's passing. Following the burial, those helping to lay the body to rest had to be cleansed from their contact with the dead. This was achieved by reciting special phrases reserved for these occasions.

... AND THEN THE EUROPEANS CAME

Before the Europeans came to California, the Chilulas lived peacefully in their small communities. Their lives and futures dramatically changed, however, after California became a state in 1850. Then it seemed as if an unending stream of Europeans were invading territory that had formerly been American Indian.

The Indians had long cherished the earth, but unfortunately the whites developed a different kind of fervor for the land. Once gold was discovered in California, hordes of miners and fortune seekers flooded the state. Hoping to become rich during the California Gold Rush, packtrains of white settlers continuously traveled through the Bald Hills and Redwood Creek region.

GOLD-HUNGRY PROSPECTORS DESPERATELY
WANTED TO STRIKE IT RICH. THEY HAD LITTLE
REGARD FOR THE INDIANS WHO HAD BEEN LIVING
THERE FOR HUNDREDS OF YEARS.

The whites looked down on the native people and viewed them suspiciously. Before long, hostilities broke out between the two groups. At times, the Indians raided and robbed the miners and packtrains crossing their terrain. The whites did more than just fight back. They adopted a policy of shooting any Indian on sight.

For a few months it looked as if the Chilulas might be able to fend off the encroaching white settlers and the soldiers protecting them. But after a while the situation changed. The Chilulas realized that there were simply too many well-armed whites determined to kill them.

The problem worsened when white pioneers, dissatisfied with the military's crusade against the Chilulas, organized their own anti-Indian campaign. They formed a volunteer group dedicated to driving these native people off the land they had lived on for centuries. Although the military was known for its brutality in dealing with the Indians, the volunteers were even worse.

The Chilulas hoped to make peace with the whites. But when a large Indian group came to meet with the white volunteer unit, the Chilulas saw that they had been tricked. Instead of working out a settlement with them, the Indians were rounded up and forced onto a boat bound for a *reservation* in another part of the state.

After several weeks of captivity, the Chilulas devised an escape plan. They had hoped to return home, but unfortunately, most never reached their destination. On the way back they were attacked by a large enemy war party of hostile Lassik Indians. Many of the Chilulas were slaughtered in the fighting.

Survivors remained in the area and joined with some neighboring Hupa and Wilkut Indians to fight the warring Lassiks. The ongoing hostilities made traveling through the region extremely perilous. Before long the packtrains and miners were careful to avoid the Bald Hills and instead sought other routes to the gold mines.

After several years, a U.S. Indian agent who had been working with the Hupas tried to solve the problem. He urged the remaining Chilula families to join the Hupas on a large reservation in Hoopa Valley, California. Having been close neighbors, the two groups' customs and beliefs were somewhat similar. And on the reservation, the Chilulas would not have to contend with either white settlers or enemy Indian attacks.

Feeling that they could never again live as they once had, most of the Chilulas agreed to make the move. But as the years passed, it seemed unlikely that

THE CHILULAS VALIANTLY FOUGHT AGAINST THE
WHITE SETTLERS WHO INVADED THEIR TERRITORY.
AFTER A TIME, THEY REALIZED THEY WERE
OUTNUMBERED AND OUTGUNNED.

SOME AMERICAN INDIANS, SUCH AS MARGARET POWELL
(SEEN HERE), CAN TRACE THEIR ROOTS BACK TO THE TIME
WHEN THE CHILULAS EXISTED AS A DISTINCT GROUP.

they would be able to maintain their distinct identity. The Chilulas had become a minority within Hupa society. And as Chilula and Hupa young people married, Chilula practices were replaced by Hupa traditions.

In time the Chilulas completely blended with the Hupas. As a result, these American Indians who once lived among the ancient redwoods no longer exist as a separate people. All that is left is their story.

GLOSSARY

Antlers the bony outgrowths on the head of an animal in the deer family.

Breechclout a piece of cloth worn by men around the hips and thighs.

Dowry the property a new wife brings to her husband at marriage.

Harpoon a long, slender barbed weapon used to catch large fish or whales.

Poultice a thick mass of healing substance applied to the skin.

Reservation a tract of land set aside by the government for Indian use.

Ritual a religious ceremony or rite.

Shaman a healer.

Sinew a strong band of tissue attaching muscle and bone.

Sweathouse a rectangular redwood structure built over a dug-out pit. It was used for sweating and purification by Chilula men.

FOR FURTHER READING

Brown, Anne Ensign. *Monarchs of the Forest: The Story of the Redwoods.* New York: Dodd, 1984.

Dixon, Ann. *How Raven Brought Light to People.* New York: Macmillan, 1992.

Eargle, Dolan H., Jr. *California Indian Country: A Guide to the Indians of California, Their Locales and Historic Sites.* San Francisco: Trees Company Press, 1986.

_____. *The Earth Is Our Mother: A Guide to the Indians of California, Their Locales and Historic Sites.* San Francisco: Trees Company Press, 1986.

Freedman, Russell. *An Indian Winter.* New York: Holiday House, 1992.

Goble, Paul. *Love Flute*. New York: Bradbury, 1992.

Lavitt, Edward, and Robert E. McDowell. *Nichancan's Feast of the Beaver: Animal Tales of the North American Indians*. Santa Fe, N. M.: Museum of New Mexico, 1990.

Shemie, Carter, ed. *Native Americans of the West: A Sourcebook on the American West*. Brookfield, Conn.: Millbrook, 1992.

White Deer of Autumn. *The Native American Book of Life*. Hillsboro, Ore. : Beyond Words, 1992.

INDEX

ABOUT THE AUTHOR

Elaine Landau has been a newspaper reporter, a children's book editor, and a youth services librarian. She has written over sixty-five books for young people, including *The Pomo, The Hopi, The Sioux,* and *The Cherokees.* Ms. Landau makes her home in Sparta, New Jersey.